P

is for

Psychic

Magick

Kitchen Table Magick Series

by
G. Alan Joel

Esoteric School of Shamanism & Magic

Email: *alan@shamanschool.com*
Website: *www.shamanschool.com*

Publisher: Esoteric School of Shamanism and Magic, Inc.

Disclaimer and Legal Notice:
The Esoteric School of Shamanism and Magic has made every effort to ensure, at the time of this writing, that the information contained in this book is as accurate as possible. The publisher and author make no warranties or representation with respect to the completeness, fitness, accuracy, applicability, or appropriateness of this book's contents. This book's information is provided strictly for entertainment and educational purposes. Should you choose to use or apply the ideas provided in this book, you take full responsibility for your own actions. The publisher and author provide no guarantee that your life will improve in any way should you choose to use the information presented in this book. The ability of the information provided in this book to provide self-help and life improvement to the reader is entirely dependent upon the reader. The reader's ability to gain positive results from the information presented in this book is entirely dependent on the amount of time the reader devotes to the application of the material in this book, the willingness of the reader to dedicate time and effort to learning the materials presented in this book, as well as the reader's own belief system, which may help or hinder the reader's ability to benefit from this book's materials. Since each reader differs according to willingness and openness to the information available in this book, the author and publisher cannot guarantee success or improvement for every individual reader. Neither the publisher nor the author assumes responsibility for the reader's actions, or whether the information is used for negative or positive purposes. The information contained in this book is drawn from tribal traditions—both modern and ancient—as well as the author's 30 plus years' experience researching and teaching this material to students. The information in this book is presented as interpreted by the author, and, as such, may or may not be entirely accurate. In no way should the information presented in this book be a substitute for advice from health or mental health professionals. The author and publisher are not liable—or in any way responsible—for actions

[this page intentionally left blank]

Psychic Magick Blessing

Child of Wonder,
Child of Flame
Nourish Our Spirits and
Protect Our Aim.

Psychic abilities be the right of all of Earth's beings,
Though some have more in the ways of seeing.
Imagination be the doorway to powers psychic,
Just open your mind... try it, you'll like it!

Pressure won't help, nor pressing need,
When it comes to psychic powers, patience you must heed.
Games and lightness are called for here,
The psychic knowings appear everywhere!

Some tools can help—dowsing rods and pendulums and
such,
But we don't need them for psychic beings help us much.
Predicting short futures will hone your psychic talents,
And "reading" others will bring forth psychic powers latent.

These simple skills be but the start,
Of a long career in the psychic arts!

The key is the enjoy, relax, and not to fear it,
While honoring the sacred knowledge with a protective
spirit.

Thus, my will, so mote it be.

[this page intentionally left blank]

Free Gift

To thank you for purchasing this book, I'd like to give you a

100% FREE GIFT

Learn more about your free magickal gift.

Access Your Free Gift at www.shamanschool.com

Find a complete list of magickal resources on https://amzn.to/3swxvPo. These resources are constantly updated so check back often!

Kitchen Table Psychic Magick
Table of Contents

[this page intentionally left blank]

Introduction to Kitchen Table Psychic Magick

"We're asking you to trust in the Well-being. In optimism there is magic."
~ Abraham

A Note About This Introduction

This book is one of a series of books in the Kitchen Table Magick series. Each book in the series addresses a specific area of magick (love, money, psychic development, etc.), and is written in a simple "recipe" format for people who want to use magick in their lives immediately. The Kitchen Table Magick series is akin to a Julia Childs recipe book, only these books contain magickal recipes for people to cook up some miraculous and magickal manifestations in their lives.

Because this series was designed so that each person could pick and choose to read just the books that pertain to their current life situation, each book is meant to be readable as a stand-alone book. To introduce the new reader to the series, this introduction to the series is repeated at the beginning of each book. If you have already read one or more books in this series, please feel free to jump ahead to the recipes that interest you. At the same time, some people feel that reviewing the introduction, as well as the "Rules and

1

Tips," is helpful before diving in. In magickal circles, your will is the guideline so choose whichever route best suits you... the Universe and magickal beings will follow!

What is Magick?

Many people have multiple different ideas about what magick is or can be. For the sake of clarity, here is what we know about magick after more than 35 years of study and practice. Magick is a precision science! It is also:

- The science of deliberate creation.
- The science of effective prayer.
- The science of manifesting Higher Will (substitute whatever Higher Force is most familiar to you) on the energetic and material planes.
- The science of heightened awareness, selective perception, and dynamic, harmonious relationships.
- The study of intention (as per Aleister Crowley, one of the greatest magickal practitioners in history).
- The system of creation, not coercion. Note: The word manipulation is often used in conjunction with magick, but manipulation simply means the use of the hands. It should be an "OK" word without a lot of charge, but currently it is used mostly to mean coercion. Look it up!
- The principle that every intentional act is a magickal act! Magick gives us the ability to communicate with beings on all levels, and allows us to understand, through direct experience, the actual workings of the Universe.
- The traditional path of spiritual growth.
- Not extraordinary knowledge. It is the "normal" way of life. We've just lost access to it. When you have this kind of knowledge in your understanding, you have the ability to resolve spiritual questions that otherwise become catechism. From a magickal point of view, catechism is not acceptable, since a practitioner must experience and verify everything for him or herself. It

2

avoids the trap of dogma. In past times, having a magickal foundation was essential so that we could talk directly to higher beings in the Universal hierarchy.

- Necessary to effective religious practice.

There is some confusion as to how to spell the word "magick." There are three different commonly used spellings: magick, magic, and majick. Eliphas Levi first used the form "magick" to differentiate religious or ceremonial from stage magick. All forms of spelling are acceptable in what this author teaches.

"I love Kitchen Table Magick! It's the best mix of both mystical and down-to-earth magick I have ever encountered. The fact that I can use items from my pantry is so handy and fun! It literally is about cooking up magic at my kitchen table, and having love show up in the least expected places!"
~ Wendy J., Skokie, IL

Is Magick Real?
Yes. Magick is very real and has existed as a precise science for thousands of years. Whether you use the word magick or another name, this spiritual practice is very real. Every single person can learn to do magick. We are ALL born with the talents and abilities that empower us to do magick. The only reason that magick seems so, well, magickal is that this society no longer teaches the art and science of magick. In the distant past, magickal study was just as important as math, science, or the arts. In fact, magick was and still is the birthright of EVERY planetary citizen.

Can you learn to do the kind of magick portrayed in the movies? Yes... and no. The movies are great at giving you a taste of what you can do with magick, but they are not very accurate. In the Harry Potter movies, for instance, the characters use their Wands for every magickal operation. In

3

reality, you can only use the Wand to handle Air energies. Your Wand would actually explode or catch fire if you tried to use it to throw Firebolts and Fireballs as the characters do in the movie.

So, what can you actually do with magick? Quite a lot. Here is a short list to get you started:

- Balance your energies for healing and manifestation
- Change old beliefs
- Defend yourself against physical and psychic attack
- Heal yourself and others
- Find hidden information and see possible futures (and change the future if you do not like the probable futures you divine)
- Psychically communicate with other beings
- Create sacred space
- Find lost people and objects
- Manifest what you want and need in life

At the very basis of magick is the understanding of the four elements: Air, Fire, Water, and Earth. Called elemental magick, these foundational elements are real. Air, Fire, Water, and Earth are part of our natural everyday environment. What makes them magickal is the understanding of how they operate not just on the physical level, but also at the levels of Mind and Spirit.

For instance, while on the physical level, Air is just the stuff we breathe. On the magickal levels Air is the conduit of psychic communication, enlightenment, understanding, dreaming, and more. If you want more of these things in your life, then you need more magickal Air. How do you get more magickal Air? Wear more Air colors, including white for communication and sky blue for enlightenment and understanding. To take this one step further, you could also use various magickal techniques to take on more Air to make your body lighter. Take on enough Air and you'll be able to levitate.

By just extending your understanding and use of the

basic ingredients of nature, you are doing magick! Seen in this light, magick isn't all smoke and mirrors, nor is it the result of Hollywood special effects. Magick is the result of truly understanding and working with the very elements that are all around you.

One final note: Many masters, including Wayne Dyer, have said, "You'll see it when you believe it." The same is true for magick. In other words, the suspension of disbelief and the willingness not to exercise contempt prior to investigation are requirements for magick to be "real." Magick is all around us, and always is, but our ability to perceive and use the forces of magick depends on our willingness to be open. No one else can show it to you, only your direct experience and observation can "prove" or demonstrate to you that magick is real.

[this page intentionally left blank]

What is Kitchen Table Magick?

Kitchen Table Magick is exactly what it sounds like—a series of simple recipes that you can literally "cook up" at your kitchen table using household ingredients from your own pantry and cupboard.

The Kitchen Table Magick books have been created for ordinary people who want to mix up a little magick in their lives without all the fancy rituals, but simply with everyday ingredients that can be found in the kitchen pantry, bathroom medicine cabinet, or even stuffed in the back of the junk drawer.

The goal of these books is to allow anyone with the desire to learn this craft to mix up magick literally at the kitchen table using simple recipes. What goes into a simple recipe?

- Everyday items as ingredients
- Easy to follow instructions that don't require years of training
- Procedures that take less than two hours from start to finish
- Built-in expertise that allows the magick to do the heavy lifting
- Some friendly advice on how you can help your magickal recipe provide the best results
- Oh, and a few little rules and guidelines about magickal practice in this specific arena that will keep you safe and sound, magickally speaking, when you use these recipes

Kitchen Table Magick Equals:
Quick – Effective – Safe – Everyday Use – Ordinary
Affordable Ingredients

Why Use Kitchen Table Magic?
- Everyone can do magick.
- Magick should be simple, effective, and start working right away, else it is not magick.
- Not everyone has the time or resources to enroll in a school.
- People ask us for magickal help in hundreds of emails everyday... Kitchen Table Magick is designed to help these very people.
- Of the many areas of life, most people only seem to need help in one or two areas, so you need only buy those Kitchen Table Magick books that apply to your needs.
- Magick is for the masses, and should be accessible, affordable, and simple to do. This is what our teacher taught us, and this is the legacy we are paying forward as well.
- While there are many more advanced forms of magick, these books are an introduction to that world so that you can dabble, experiment, try things out, see the result, adjust and amend, and generally have fun... just as you would cooking a meal in your kitchen.
- This book is not for the major foodie, but is perfect for the person who needs magickal help right here, right now!

Who Should Use These Recipes?
- You and anyone you know who would like a little more magick and a little less ordinary reality in their lives.
- Anyone who needs help RIGHT now and doesn't have time to fly to India or Sedona to sit at the feet of a guru.

- Anyone who does not have access to anything but a computer for help and guidance.
- Anyone who wants to do magick and then forget it (all while quietly watching the magick "do its thing").
- Anyone who wants affordable, down to earth magick they can do with regular ingredients in the comfort of home.

When to Use Kitchen Table Magic: Anytime...

- You need help.
- You don't want to do all the heavy lifting (leave that to the Angels, Spirit Guides, Animal Totems, and so forth).
- You seem stuck in a rut or corner with no way out.
- You've been struggling with a problem for a long time and need a resolution.
- You don't know what to do but you need to do SOMETHING.
- You'd like to learn how to practice the craft.
- You want to live a more magickal life and stop dealing with ordinary hassles all the time.

How Do We Know These Recipes Work?

- We teach a slew of these recipes in one-day workshops all over the country, via teleconference, and via videoconference. We also email them to people as part of our school's service work, or post them on our blogs and articles library.
- We have used them for over 35 years and still do, every single day – literally tested out at our own kitchen tables for over 35 years (and at thousands of kitchen tables around the world) for a quarter century or more.
- We receive all kinds of stories and testimonials from happy successful students.

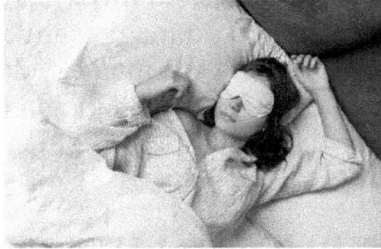

Kitchen Table Psychic Magick at Work...

Read the following example to discover how Psychic Magick works in real life...

Worry-Free Napping in Airports

I used to love to travel, but after the pandemic, not so much. Traveling these days has become a restless game of "hurry up and, oops, wait!" Sometimes the airlines overbook flights, cancel flights, or cease to fly from some hubs altogether, traveling by plane has become really tedious!

Being a business traveler in sales, I really don't have the option to not travel by plane. So, I've spent a lot of time in airports lately. Not fun. Luckily, I was taking a course in Psychic Development from the Esoteric School. We were playing with honing our psychic skills with various games that involved using our psychic powers to "read" people around us, more than we could find out via our five senses.

There were two particular games we played: one involved "telling a story" about a random person using our psychic skills (and imagination); the other was about putting up a "psychic perimeter" around ourselves, closing our eyes, and sensing when someone crossed our "psychic" lines.

The first game was fun, but I got more mileage out of the perimeter game while waiting for flights at various airports around the world. The "psychic story" game was difficult to validate because most people are wary and have more fear in airports. Walking up and trying to ask questions to validate or invalidate our psychic data would have seemed suspicious. So, I stuck with the perimeter game.

This game was actually pretty useful. I'm often tired when traveling and like to take short naps whenever I can. In an airplane, I have quite a bit of control over my "stuff" because my bags are either at my feet or work on my body. Even if I put bags in an overhead bin, the sound of the bin opening usually wakes me up.

Airports are a different story. Airports are noisy, busy with foot traffic, and riskier in terms of getting items stolen. But I still wanted to be able to cat nap. So, the perimeter game was perfect. I would sit down in the least crowded place I could find in the waiting area and set my bags down around my feet. After setting up a psychic perimeter, I would program the perimeter to wake me up whenever someone crossed my psychic boundaries. Then I would close my eyes and take a nap.

At first, my five senses would take over—I would wake up every time I heard footsteps or voices or felt the seat shift when someone sat down near me. With practice I learned to close down my five senses and float in a semi-conscious state. At first, I still woke up often, even when no one had crossed my boundaries. But after consciously putting more trust in the Universe, I was able to truly nap, and only awaken when my psychic circle was broken.

What started out as a slightly frustrating exercise (it does take some practice), but now this is my "go to" magickal trick whenever I travel. I trust my psychic skills because my experience has shown me that they work, very well! I now sleep like a baby at airports and have never had a single item stolen from me. Pretty neat trick!

~ John L., Fort Lauderdale, FL

A Few Rules and Tips About Kitchen Table Magick

As with any game, the game of life has its own set of rules. Specifically, the spiritual side of life has rules. Play by those rules and you will stay safe and easily attract what you want into your life. Break those rules and all types of unwanted consequences happen.

These "spiritual rules" are ones that have been observed, both in personal spiritual practice and spiritual practice with various associated groups and teachers. These rules universally govern any spiritual practice, and appear to be in effect whether you know them or not. Unlike ethics and morals, which change with culture and time, these spiritual rules appear to have remained the same throughout time, unchanging, like physical and scientific rules.

The rules in the following section are adapted from *Rules of the Road*, as created by George Dew, co-founder of the Church of Seven Arrows. There are two major rules, which are common to most spiritual practices, along with some minor rules that are specific to our form of magickal practice.

Two Major Rules

These two rules will probably sound familiar, as they appear in most major religions and spiritual practices, most probably because they are common-sense and apply not just to spiritual practice, but to life as well.

First Rule: Golden Rule or Law of Karma
This first rule is literally a "golden oldie":

What you do to the environment or to other beings in the environment brings similar effects back to you in your life.

Often recognized as the Golden Rule or the Law of Karma, this rule tops the list because it reminds all spiritual practitioners of potential unwanted "rebound" or side effects. As your spiritual power, focus, and abilities grow, this rule will have an ever-greater impact on your life unless you exercise caution. The Universe responds more strongly and powerfully to those with focus, power, and ability.

Note: As humanity moves further in the Aquarian Age, many spiritual practitioners have seen more effects from this rule occur faster. In the past, effects of this rule that often took lifetimes to manifest now occur in minutes, days, weeks, or months. In this particular time in Earth's history, karma seems to operate under a "pay as you go" system. Simply stated, expect the effects of the Law of Karma to occur quickly.

Second Rule: The Judgment of "Good and Bad" According to the Universe
This second rule adds clarity and detail to the first rule described previously:

If you are unsure whether your acts are "good or bad"-- that is, whether those acts are in keeping with universal laws on this planet—the Universe will reflect its judgment back to you quickly, according to the "pay as you go" Law of Karma.

This law holds as true for individuals as it does for entire communities, states, nations, or other organized groups. If you are still unsure of the feedback you receive from the Universe, check areas such as your level of health, the soundness of social relationships, your prosperity or lack of, sufficiency of various needs in life, and even your "luck" with appliances and machines. If your luck appears to be consistently poor, then you are probably acting contrary to universal governing laws, regardless of your intentions. The Universe cares about what you do more than what you intend.

Additional Detailed Rules

The following rules offer more detailed standards by which to measure your acts or the acts of others to determine whether these acts are in accordance with universal laws.

- Do nothing that will harm another being unless you are willing to suffer similar or greater harm. What the Universe considers "harm" may be different than what you consider harm.
- Do not bind another being unless you are willing to be similarly bound. An example of binding someone is doing acts in attempt to coerce a specific other person to love you. There is no problem with attracting your soul mate into your life, but doing acts that attempt to coerce a specific other person to love you is a type of binding.
- Never use your spiritual abilities in vain, to show off, or to boost your pride. Using your spiritual abilities from a place of pride usually causes the Universe to bring instant backlash into your life.
- If you choose to charge money or barter for using your spiritual abilities in the service of others, avoid charging extremely high prices. Charge prices for using methods comparable to other professionals, such as an attorney or accountant.
- Never use any spiritual word, chant, litany, or similar "device" unless you are confident in your understanding of its methods, intents, and effects.
- When undertaking a major spiritual operation—one that will require significant effort or attempts to create a major effect in the world—use divination to

determine whether you can safely benefit from such an operation, and to discover the obstacles you must overcome. Divination methods such as pendulum readings, channeling, meditation, and question circles (to name a few) can reveal hidden factors of which you may be unaware.

- In any spiritual endeavor, take your time, think it through, and do it right!

The good news is that you can still do psychic magick rituals. The ones we teach in this book won't get you in trouble with the Universe while also allowing you to strengthen your natural psychic abilities. With enough practice, you'll soon learn to extend past your five psychical senses and begin tapping into your Spirit senses.

The Ingredients of Psychic Magick

"If you are resisting anything, you are focused upon it, pushing against it, and activating the vibration of it – and therefore attracting that which is like it."
~ Abraham Hicks

Psychic development is a study of the advanced use of our spirit perceptics, our Spirit's abilities. Furthermore, it is an introduction to soul consciousness and our awareness of soul function in us—how to awaken ourselves to it so that, as Alice Bailey tells us, "We are soul-led." The recipes presented in this book will lead you to investigate and determine—what are the properties and capabilities of a soul—when, where, and how it functions. They will also help you to begin accessing information that you can't possibly know through your five senses. One of the keys to success in developing these abilities is learning to ignore the outcome. Just practice your abilities and don't worry about whether you're "right" or not. The "art of ignoring" or selective perception is one of the key principles in magick and in developing your psychic abilities. Remember, you're accessing information in another realm, so you have to learn to focus your attention in that realm. Putting your attention solely on asking and receiving is the key.

Everyone is Psychic—That Means You!

We are familiar with our five bodily senses of touch, taste, sound, sight, and scent. What we rarely consider is our Spirit senses, how Spirit receives information directly from the world around us, neither from body nor from mind, allowing us first-hand experience. Every single person on this planet has psychic abilities. There is not a single person who doesn't. Psychic abilities are the birthright of every citizen on this planet—we just forget to use those abilities regularly so they grow weak.

The difference between people who are "psychic" and people who are not is often just a matter of practice. Obviously there are people who are naturally more tuned-in to psychic wavelengths than others, but there are also many other psychics who simply practice, refine, and verify their abilities with regular exercises, including the ones we present in the recipes in this book. If you want to increase your psychic abilities, you can with the upcoming recipes. The best news is that these psychic exercises are very simple and can be done very easily in public without anyone noticing what you are doing.

If you've tried various methods to increase your psychic abilities but they haven't worked, don't despair. With every recipe you work your way through, we help you troubleshoot problem areas. If there is a psychic brick wall, we've run into it ... many times! So we understand the frustration of our psychic skills being less than spectacular, but we've also found lots of ways to get around those brick walls. One of the keys to success in developing your psychic abilities is learning to ignore the outcome. Just practice your abilities and don't worry about whether you're "right" or not. After all that's why it is called "practice". Just like when you practice the piano, you are not going to be a concert pianist right off the bat.

A Word to Those About to Embark on This Path

Although it is suggested that the recipes in this book

be followed to the best of one's ability, this is a self-determined course of study. What that means is that you must act according to your own needs and aim in determining how much time you will devote to doing these exercises, how consistent your practice will be, and how willing you are to do things in a new and different way. There are no competitions, no grades, no tests other than what you require of yourself. Our aim—in offering this information—is to be supportive, non-judgmental, but encouraging in that you will amaze yourself in the discovery of both who you are and who you are not. As always, altered procedures produce altered results. All that we do shall be guided by "Rules of the Road" and the operating laws of this Universe, so as long as these guidelines be followed, no one will ever be put "at risk" in anything that we undertake.

A Word on the "Inconvenience Factor"

Part of the function of life is to produce challenge, which most often we see as resistance and obstacles. The function of creating rituals in life, from the shamanic viewpoint, is to have sacred space – to insulate ourselves from resistance and distraction so we can explore our world, to investigate our own psychic awareness and abilities.

It has been our observation, through the teaching of many classes, that students usually encounter the "inconvenience factor" when beginning studies such as these. Undertaking studies such as these requires you to make many small and some radical changes in your life. This often attracts a resistance that manifests as situations occurring to make continuing study inconvenient. For some people, it manifests in the inability to get to class because of a sudden bout of phone or car trouble, relatives unexpectedly coming to visit, work hours becoming radically increased, or unforeseen travel. For others, family or career demands suddenly become "too much" and "something must give." For others, some drastic event occurs in their life.
All those who have pushed through the inconvenience and finished the course have found their lives radically improved,

no matter the temporarily inconvenient conditions in which they found themselves. You will have to make the choice of which is more important – your magickal study or convenience. In making your choice, remember this: while magick studies may be highly inconvenient, when applied properly, they can greatly reduce the level of struggle and increase the level of joy in your life.

At the beginning of your magickal journey you will be able to straddle the two worlds, mundane and magickal, sometimes choosing mundane convenience and sometimes choosing magick. However, as you progress in your studies and your intention grows in strength and force, the two worlds will diverge more and more. At some point, you will need to make a choice between the two worlds – magickal or mundane? You will know when you have reached that point.

A Word on Partners

Over the years we have observed that students taking our Psychic Development course with friends, partners, significant others, or students who find partners once they start the course generally have much better results. Therefore, if you are not embarking on this study together with someone you know, whom you can practice with, we suggest you find one or two people who would be willing to work with you on the new information you will receive through these recipes. It is easy, especially in the beginning, to become overwhelmed with the daily tasks of life and forget to do our magickal practice. Having one or more partners to check in with throughout the week will help you remember that you are engaged in magickal study. Plus, having partners makes this study much more engaging and fun!

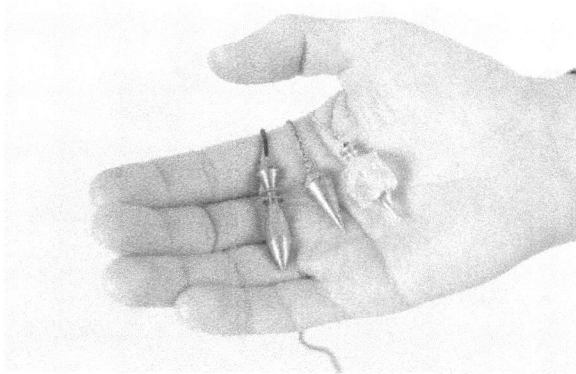

Psychic Magick Appetizer Recipes

Appetizers: Simple Magickal Ways to Develop Your Psychic Abilities

Use Dowsing Rods to Develop Psychic Abilities

Use the Pendulum to Develop Your Psychic Abilities

"The universe is full of magical things, patiently waiting for our wits to grow sharper."
~ Eden Phillpotts

[this page intentionally left blank]

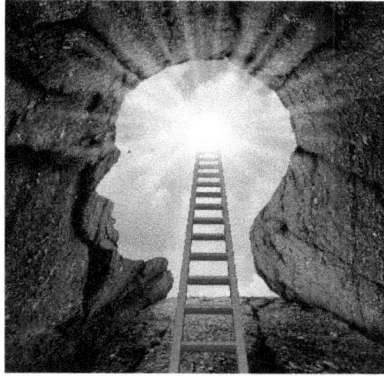

Use Dowsing Rods to Develop Psychic Abilities

"The intellect has little to do on the road to discovery. There comes a leap in consciousness, call it Intuition or what you will, the solution comes to you and you don't know how or why."
~ Albert Einstein

Time Required: Sixty Minutes

Dowsing is a powerful psychic technique as well as a form of divination. Divination is the means of obtaining information by psychic or magickal means that is not readily available to the five senses of the body. One of the ways to dowse is with the use of a Y-shaped wooden rod or with L-rods. L-rods can be made using 2 metal coat hangers and a drinking straw and is the type we will include directions for making in this set of recipes. After making your L-rods, you will find recipes for using them to develop psychic abilities.

Making L-Rods
Ingredients
- Coat hanger made completely of metal (no cardboard pieces)
- Drinking straw
- Measuring tape
- Scissors
- Wire-cutting pliers

Recipe Directions
1. Use the pliers to cut the curved top of the hanger just below the twisted section of wire (this will require two cuts). This will leave you with one piece of wire with two bends.

2. Now measure the longest section of the metal piece and mark the halfway point.

3. Use your pliers to snip the hanger where you made your mark. Now you have two pieces of wire, each with a bend.

4. Reshape each piece of wire so that each wire has a 90 degree bend.

5. Take one of the metal pieces and measure both lengths of metal on either side of the curve. Snip both the short and long lengths so that the long length is three times as long as the short length. For example, if the short length is 3 inches then the long length should be 9 inches.

6. Do the same for the other rod.

7. Using the scissors, snip a piece from the drinking straw so that the straw is slightly shorter than the short side of the rod.

8. Slide the drinking straw over the short side of the rod, then use the pliers to bend the end of the rod so that the straw can't slide off. The straw allows you to hold the rod while allowing it to swing freely.

9. Repeat the process to make your second rod.

How to Use the Results of Your Recipe

You now have your own pair of homemade dowsing rods! To begin practicing with your rods, you will need to first train them with the following directions.

Training Your Dowsing Rods

Like all magical tools, for your dowsing rods to be most effective, you need to personalize and "train" them to work for you.

Ingredients
- Plain white sheet of paper
- Something to draw with
- Open area of several feet in your house

Recipe Directions
1. Take a sheet of plain white paper and draw a large "X" that takes up the entire page.

2. Place the page in the center of an open area of your house.

3. Step away from the paper and stand at least 5 feet away, facing the "X."

4. Hold one dowsing rod in each hand, angling your hands so that the rods point straight ahead of you.

5. Remain standing still and command your dowsing rods: "Find the X!"

6. Keep your mind focused on finding the X as you walk toward the X on the ground. Carefully keep your hands neutral and don't try to control the process. As you walk closer to the X, the ends of your rods should begin to move towards each other. They should cross each other as you walk over the X. As you walk away from the X, the rods should move away from each other again.

How to Use the Results of Your Recipe

Don't worry if your rods don't "find" the X at first. Remember, this exercise is meant to help you train your dowsing rods. Just keep practicing this exercise, approaching the X from different angles. Once your dowsing rods cross reliably as you walk over the X, it is time to move onto the next exercise for practicing dowsing with your rods - dowsing your own aura - which you will find in the following recipe.

<u>Dowsing Auras with L-Rods</u>

Dowsing your own aura is simple as long as you have been practicing the training recipe above with your dowsing rods.

Ingredients
- Your L-Rods
- Full-length mirror or the largest mirror you have access to
- (Optional) A partner to dowse auras with

Recipe Directions
1. Stand about 10 feet from the mirror holding your dowsing rods.

2. Command your rods: "Show me where my aura begins."

3. Begin walking slowly toward the mirror until you see your rods cross. The place where the rods cross is the outer edge of your aura.

4. If at first your dowsing rods do not cross, back up and do it again. Remember to relax—this is not a test! Once it works for you, back up and change the exercise.

5. This time, program the dowsing rods by saying "Do not show me where my aura begins!" and then walk toward the mirror. Your rods, this time, should not cross.

6. If you choose to do the option of practicing dowsing with a partner, your partner will first need to make their own set of dowsing rods and use the X on the paper recipe to train it and program it to their own energies.

7. To dowse your partner's aura or let them dowse yours, face the person standing 10 to 15 feet away and command your rods to find the edge of their aura.

8. Then begin walking slowly towards the person until your rods cross. Repeat the process from both sides of the person and from behind them as a person's aura often varies in size on different areas around the body.

9. After practicing successfully with auras, you can start practicing dowsing for items by using small items placed around your house or outside property and following the same procedure as for dowsing auras.

How to Use the Results of Your Recipe

Keep practicing this exercise until you can reliably find the edge of your aura or keep your rods neutral by commanding them not to locate the edge of your aura. When you dowse your own aura in the mirror, you will only be able to dowse your aura from the front. In most people, the aura is not uniform on all sides of the body. If you work with a partner and dowse each other's auras, you will be able to see how far your aura extends on each side. You can use your L-rods to dowse for anything. This is especially useful for finding lost objects. The more you practice and program your L-rods, the more accurate they will become. And the only way to know that you are correctly programming your dowsing rods is by dowsing verifiable items. If you really want to challenge yourself, have your partner hide an object without revealing what it is. You can then look for "the object that [your partner's name here] has hidden on this property." This is a good beginning way to start using your Spirit senses to get information you cannot get with your physical five senses as you use a physical tool as an interface.

Use the Pendulum to Develop Your Psychic Abilities

"Human kind gradually begins to remove the blinders from their consciousness about life, about what is real and what is not. Intuition and psychic abilities increase."
~ Elaine Seiler

Time Required: Sixy Minutes

You can make a pendulum from almost any lightweight object such as paper clips, small rocks, earrings, hairpins, pendants, small medallions, or crystals and talismans suspended on a chain, string, or thread. If you choose to use a crystal, use an amethyst. Other types of crystals, especially quartz crystals, are too easily contaminated by negative energies. Store any kind of crystal you use as a magickal tool in a pewter box, which protects it from contamination. Don't use Aurora crystals, which have been treated with petroleum. If you choose to hang your pendulum on a chain, use a silver chain; silver is a very stable element with very few side bands. Don't use a gold chain; gold is a power color and is much less stable with too many side bands. You can also hang your pendulum on any kind of natural fiber such as cotton or silk, horse or human hair, or leather. You can also buy a pendulum at new age type stores or online.

After you make or buy a pendulum, you will need to key it to your own energies and train or program it like you would with other magickal tools. This recipe will show you how to do this as well as how to begin using your pendulum to clear negative or repetitive thoughts you may have or problem areas in your life. Clearing these types of conditions with a pendulum helps you be in a place of receiving for information from the higher and for using your psychic abilities.

Ingredients
- A pendulum
- Printed copies of the indicator plates provided below
- Plate (magickal Earth energy tool) made of wood, ceramic, or porcelain decorated with earth tone colors or with plant-based designs that is 6 – 10 inches in diameter
- Charged Sun Yellow candle
- Grass Green color source
- Wooden or paper matches
- (optional) Two white candles
- A list of questions about the near future (that can be verified within an hour's time)

Recipe Directions
1. Key your pendulum by holding it in your output hand (usually the hand you use to point with) and flow energy into it until it feels hot, charged, or tingly. These sensations indicate that your pendulum is keyed.

2. Light a Sun candle and charge it sitting in the South facing North cupping your hands above the flame and saying in a voice of command:

"Child of Wonder
Child of Flame
Nourish My Spirit
And Protect My Aim."

3. Quick-key your plate by holding it in both hands and running Grass Green energy from your dominant hand (the one you point with) through the plate to your other hand. Circle the Green energy up your arm, around your shoulders, and back down to your dominant hand. Keep this energy circuit flowing until the plate feels keyed (usually a minute or two). The plate may feel electric, heavier, or tingly.

4. Put a copy of the paper indicator plate that will best answer your question on your Plate.

5. You can also put two Sun Yellow or White protection candles on either side of your Plate. The candle on the right is the Wisdom candle and protects the reading from your own influences. The candle on the left is the Protection candle and prevents anyone else from impacting the reading.

6. If you choose to use the protection candles, light a wooden or paper match, using it to light the right candle. Bring the same lit match down and across your plate to light the left candle. Then bring the same lit match up and across your plate to touch the flame of the right candle again. This procedure causes the two candles to trade auras and creates a field of protection over your divination.

7. Form a tripod with your body by placing your elbows on the table on either side of the Plate, inside the candles. Your two arms form two legs of the tripod and your body forms the third leg. This is the "indirect" method of using a pendulum which means you cannot move your arms or hands to influence the swing. The "direct" method of using the pendulum allows it to swing freely in one hand, but our own hopes, fears, beliefs, and thoughts can easily influence the results as the direct method has no interference controls.

8. Place the chain of your pendulum through the gap between your thumb and index finger of one hand and lace your hands together so that the chain ends up suspended between your two thumb mounds. Make sure the pendulum can swing freely.

9. Position your arms and body so that the pendulum hangs straight down over the center of the indicator plate. Don't swing the pendulum; it will begin to swing on its own.

10. Form a question and hold it in your mind. You can also speak the question out loud.

11. The pendulum will begin to swing on its own. If it moves in a clockwise direction, keep holding the question as your focus – the answer is coming. If the pendulum moves in a counterclockwise direction, you are trying too hard but not focusing on the question. It indicates that you are speculating on the answer or that you are distracted. Take a deep breath and refocus your attention.

12. Once the pendulum is swinging in a clockwise motion, it will then begin to swing in a line. Observe the line carefully as there will be a long leg and a short leg.

The direction of the longer leg is your answer.

13. Continue asking questions from your list of "short futures". These "short futures" questions will teach your pendulum to be accurate. For instance, you might ask your pendulum, "Will my housemate come home within the next 15 minutes?", "Will my phone ring within 30 minutes?", "Will my client be late for our 3:00 appointment?" and so on.

14. With this method of using the pendulum, you can get any information you want from the Universe. Don't be discouraged if all your answers are not accurate in the beginning. It takes some time to align the energies of your pendulum and yourself and the more you practice, the more reliable your answers will be.

15. If you find yourself fretting or having negative thoughts that could be interfering with life in general or with the use of your pendulum for receiving information, you can use the direct method with your pendulum to clear away these types of energies.

16. To use the pendulum in this way, dangle your pendulum from your dominant hand (you do not need to use the tripod method) while you visualize a current life problem or focus on the negative thoughts or energy that is affecting you.

17. Use the Yes-No indicator plate to ask your pendulum, "Can I, may I, should I, clear this situation?" If your pendulum says, "yes," then proceed.

18. Begin to swing the pendulum in a counterclockwise direction as you ask the pendulum to clear the situation. "See" the situation resolving in your mind. Be as specific as possible in your request to your pendulum, and envision the situation being resolved.

19. Keep focusing on clearing the situation until your pendulum stops spinning counterclockwise. Your pendulum will either start moving along the vertical or horizontal axis, stop, or start spinning clockwise. When your pendulum stops swinging of its own accord, the trouble has been cleared.

20. Trust the power of your intent (and your pendulum) and release the problem from your consciousness. If you find yourself thinking about the problem during the day, change your focus to something else ... like a pink elephant!

How to Use the Results of Your Recipe

Choose the indicator plate that will best serve to give you an answer to the type of question you ask. With the Yes-No plate, there are also the options of Maybe Yes and Maybe No. Either of these indicate a 70% probability of Yes or No, but also that there could be problems and more research needs to be done. For instance, an answer of Maybe Yes indicates that you should probably proceed, but that there may be problems and you need to ask more questions to get more information.

Pendulum Indicator Plates:

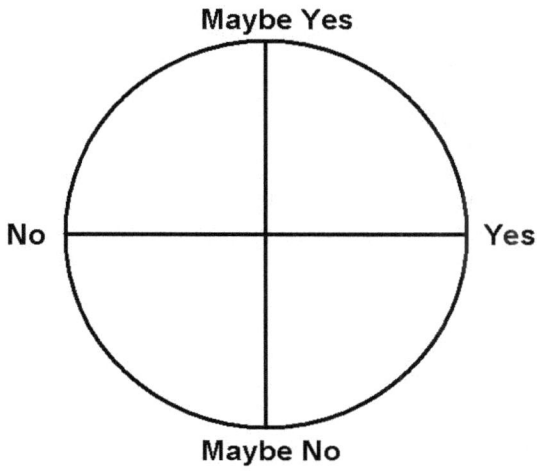

Maybe Yes

No — Yes

Maybe No

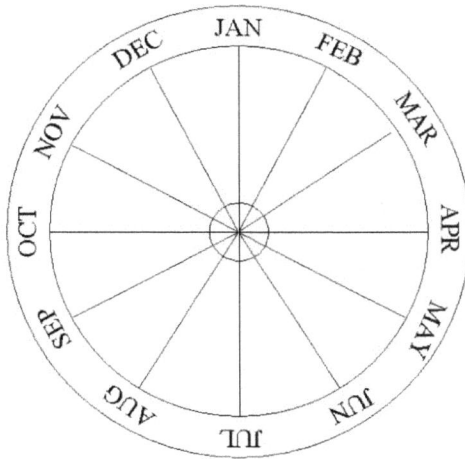

JAN FEB MAR APR MAY JUN JUL AUG SEP OCT NOV DEC

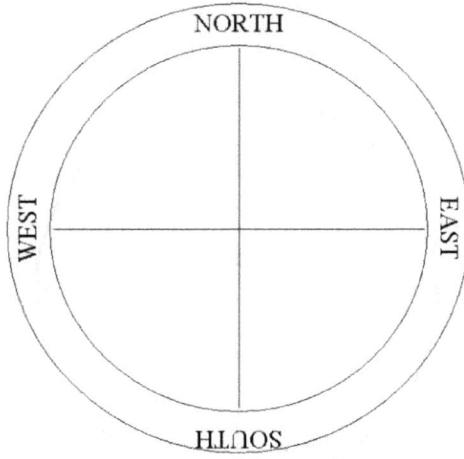

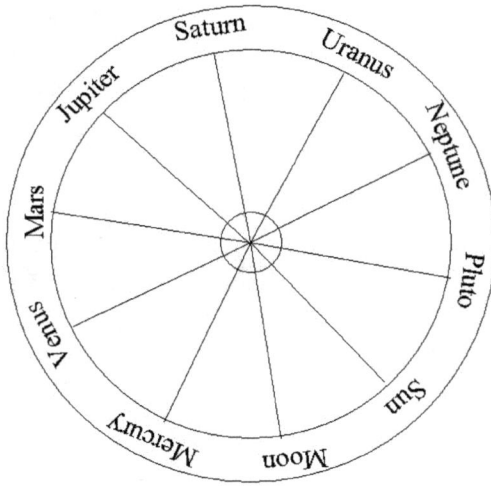

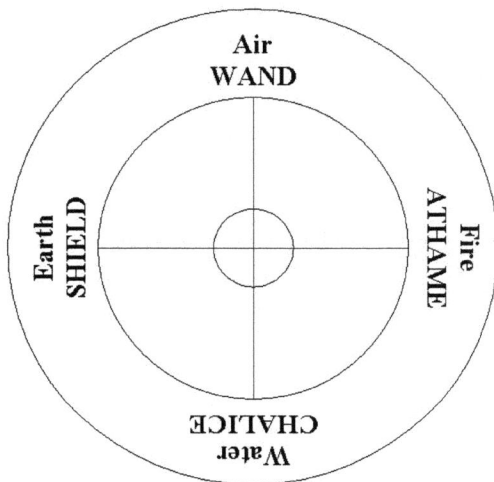

[this page intentionally left blank]

Psychic Magick Main Course Recipes

Main Courses: Receiving Information From the Universe

Learn to Psychically Read People in Public Places

Predict Daily Short Futures

The Psychic Perimeter Game

"Psychic power is the ability to download information directly from the Universe."
~ Lada Ray

[this page intentionally left blank]

Learn to Psychically Read People in Public Places

"Take the first step in faith. You don't have to see the whole staircase. Just take the first step."
~ Dr Martin Luther King Jr.

Time Required: Five Minutes

This recipe allows you to practice using your Spirit abilities to access information that you can't access with your five senses.

Ingredients
- Pen
- Blank paper
- A watch or timer
- A location that gives you access to many people

Recipe Directions

1. Bring pen, paper, and a watch or timer to a very public location that has lots of people. Fast food restaurants, airports, or malls are good places to start.

2. Seat yourself in a comfortable location where you can easily write, observe people, and see your timer or clock.

3. Pick a person to observe (you will need to observe them for 30 seconds). Set your timer for 30 seconds and start writing.

4. Write anything and everything that comes up about that person, whether you can directly observe it or not. It's easier to start by writing what you can observe about the person (such as hair color, clothing, activities and so forth). Don't think about what you are writing and don't allow yourself time to pause. Don't worry about whether your observations are correct or not. Write as much as you can and as fast as you can.

5. Once the 30 seconds is up, pick another person to observe, set your timer, and start writing.

6. Observe 10 people during a span of 5 minutes.

7. Your writing about each person may look something like: "Man, blond hair, jeans, has kids, mustache, kind, loves sports, likes water, has a brother, works outdoors, in tune with Nature, born in the West or has a connection to the West, nice tan, sneakers, talking with someone, talks with hand gestures, works well with hands, sensitive hands, sensitive nature, enjoys people, likes the color red, wears red a lot, brown eyes, around 40, likes jazz music, smiles a lot."

8. In this example, you see there are many descriptions that can be seen with the five senses – the color of his hair, the way he talks with his hands, the color of his eyes and his tan. In between, though, are descriptors that can't be seen with the five senses – that he has a brother, he is in tune with Nature, likes the color red and jazz music. These are what you have picked up through your Spirit abilities.

How to Use the Results of Your Recipe

It doesn't matter if any of your descriptions, especially those that are done with Spirit abilities, are actually correct. The goal is to practice accessing information with these abilities. The correctness of your observations will improve with time. There is also no need at this point to verify your observations, just note them and move on. This is time devoted to practice and verifying accuracy is not necessary and could cause you to bring doubt into your practice. Just keep chugging along practicing this exercise as often as you can – any time you are waiting for a bus, sitting at a restaurant, or resting in a public setting. If you don't get out much, you can do the same exercise by turning the volume off your TV and observing the people on TV. The more you practice, the better your psychic abilities will get. You will find as you progress and become more skilled at the use of your psychic abilities that you will begin "reading" people from a wider angle view of them. You will begin taking in impressions from their auras, body movements, what they are doing with their hands and feet, how they are breathing, the color of the tongue, how their eyes look, what their posture is like, the types of parenthetical statements they make and all sorts of other information about them that comes from Spirit's perceptic inputs and is plugged into our mind's computer system to give us a printout of information about that person.

The key is to not stop and think about what to write; just let the words flow through you onto the paper with whatever pops out.

[this page intentionally left blank]

Predict Daily Short Futures

"Built into you is an internal guidance system that shows you the way home. All you need to do is heed the voice."
~ Neale Donald Walsh

Time Required: Five Minutes

This recipe is another way that allows you to practice accessing information that you can't possibly know through your five senses. Again, don't worry about your accuracy in the beginning. This is a practice exercise to hone your skills that gets you in the practice of asking for information from a higher level of consciousness and listening for the answers.

Ingredients

- Ideas for questions you can ask about short futures (verifiable in less than an hour)

Recipe Directions

1. As you go about your day each day, be aware of situations you encounter that you could ask a question about. For example, before walking into a movie theater ask yourself how many people will already be sitting in the theater when you walk in. Pause and listen to the first answer you hear and don't question it or think any more about it.

2. Thank your inner being and/or the Universe for the answer.

3. Now here's the hard part for many people. Walk into the theater and DO NOT count the people sitting there. In fact, act as if you hadn't ever asked the question.

4. Avoiding verification of your answers will allow you to be more open to what your psychic abilities tell you (rather than hearing all your own doubtful mind chatter). You will eventually begin to notice how "right on" your abilities are—if you can actually avoid verification of your answers early on in the process.

5. Continue looking for situations that you can ask questions about and using the same procedure. Maybe you are about to walk into a store and could ask questions like "What's the biggest discount being offered today?", "What is the most unusual color you'll see in the store?", or "Will you meet anyone you know in the store?".

6. Again, the key is not to put your attention on verifying your answer. Just keep asking the question, receiving the first answer you get, thanking yourself and/or the Universe for the answer, and ignoring the rest.

How to Use the Results of Your Recipe

Over time, you will unavoidably begin noticing the "correctness" of your answers. You can't help but notice that you've picked out the highest discount a store is offering or that you actually did meet someone you know in the mall. The "art of ignoring" or selective perception is one of the key principles in magick and in developing your psychic abilities. Remember, you're accessing information in another realm, so you have to learn to focus your attention in that realm. Putting your attention solely on asking and receiving is the key.

[this page intentionally left blank.]

The Psychic Perimeter Game

"Close both eyes to see with the other"
~ Rumi

Time Required: Thirty Minutes Per Day

Another way to sharpen your psychic skills and gain information not readily available to the five senses is to shut off one of your five senses. For instance, you can close your eyes to stop receiving visual data. You can then practice "reading" the psychic information around you. The game presented in this recipe allows you to do this by having you set up an energetic or psychic perimeter around yourself in a public place. Just close your eyes and imagine an energy circle surrounding you. You then notice, without using your eyes, whenever someone steps inside that perimeter.

Ingredients
- A location in public that you can observe other people around you

Recipe Directions

1. At least once a day (and obviously not while doing something such as driving) set up an energetic perimeter around yourself of about 10 – 20 feet preferably in a public place such as a park, restaurant, outdoor café, or bus stop.

2. Close your eyes and in your "mind's eye" see a circle of energy surrounding you.

3. Sit quietly and focus on your circle. Be aware of anytime someone enters your perimeter area.

4. When you have the sense that someone has entered your area, open your eyes to confirm it.

How to Use the Results of Your Recipe

Once you play this psychic game enough that you are getting accurate at sensing someone entering your area, gradually you may increase the size of your circle. You might also move on to taking another of your five senses out of the equation like by playing this game in a noisy environment to avoid using your hearing to check when someone crosses into your circle. You'll notice that the more you practice this psychic exercise and the more of your physical senses you can avoid using, the more sensitive your psychic abilities will be.

Psychic Magick Dessert Recipes

Desserts: Whipped Cream with a Cherry on Top!

Create a Psychic Magick Talisman

Send a Message with Firebowl

"We have two ears and one mouth so that we can listen twice as much as we speak"
~ Epictetus

[this page intentionally left blank]

Create a Psychic Magick Talisman

"The concept of psychic energy is easy for most people to imagine. After all, it's just one step beyond intuition – and almost everyone is comfortable with the idea of intuition."
~ Jayne Ann Krentz

Time Required: Sixty Minutes

When first starting to work with the Universe to receive information not available through the five physical senses, many people let their minds "get in the way" and set up blocks that prevent them from receiving information. Until one is more secure in working with the Universe in this way and is able to overcome the "doubt factor", using a magick talisman can be helpful.

Ingredients
- A bright yellow Sun candle with no orange or reddish undertones

- A plate for fire safety with the candle or use a candle enclosed in glass
- Wooden or paper matches
- A talisman that symbolizes your request to the Universe (and is small enough to carry around all day)
- A pen and notebook to record your magickal work (also called a Book of Shadows)
- A compass to find the exact location of the cardinal directions

Recipe Directions

1. Locate the four cardinal directions by using your compass outdoors. Compasses do not give accurate readings indoors as there is too much electro-magnetic interference. Once you have located all the directions, go back in your house and clear a small circular space.

2. Bring all your materials and sit in the South of the circle, placing your items in front of you.

3. Place your Sun candle in front of you (on the plate if necessary) and light the candle with a wooden or paper match. Do not use a lighter as lighter fluid has unwanted energies.

4. Once the flame of the candle is burning tall and bright (called a working flame), cup your hands around the flame and say the following litany in a voice of command:

> *"Child of Wonder*
> *Child of Flame*
> *Nourish My Spirit*
> *And Bring My Aim"*

5. Now hold the talisman you selected in your dominant hand (the hand you use to point). As you hold the

talisman, focus on the energy of being open-minded, serene, filled with wonder and awe, and joyful. Focus on how you will feel knowing that you are working with the Universe and are able to receive information and messages not available to you through your five physical senses. Flow all the positive and joyful energy you can access into the talisman. When the talisman feels charged, hot, energized, heavy, or simply different, the talisman is keyed to you and to your desire to communicate with higher powers and beings.

6. Now place the talisman next to or around the candle (an example might be using a talisman that is a heart locket on a chain or a small figure of a spirit animal such as Owl) and say the following verse in a voice of command:

"Child of Wonder
Child of Flame
Energize This Talisman
With Magick Untamed
Each Time I Touch This Talisman
The Energies of Mundane and Magickal Combine
My Energies Through the Talisman Aid
This Spell That Manifests My Desires So Fine."

7. Leave the talisman near the burning Sun candle (perhaps on a plate or in the sink for safety) for 30 minutes. Then blow out the candle and carry the talisman with you all day. Whenever you feel doubt about the Universe delivering on your request for information, touch your talisman for a magickal boost. Similarly, when you feel positive and happy, flow that energy into the talisman to add energy to matrix surrounding it.

8. You may repeat the keying/charging of the talisman at

any time, and many people like to repeat this process a few times to fully keep the energy flowing around it.

How to Use the Results of Your Recipe

Ask the Universe for help or ask for information or guidance then carry your talisman with you throughout the day as a physical reminder to be aware of signs, symbols, and information as it comes in from a multitude of sources. You may open a magazine to a particular article, hear a song on the radio, overhear a conversation by two passing strangers or receive the information you are looking for in a million other similar ways. Your talisman being keyed to facilitating the energetic flow of information and communication will help you open your mind to becoming aware of these types of communications from the Universe as you are developing a relationship with this type of higher power.

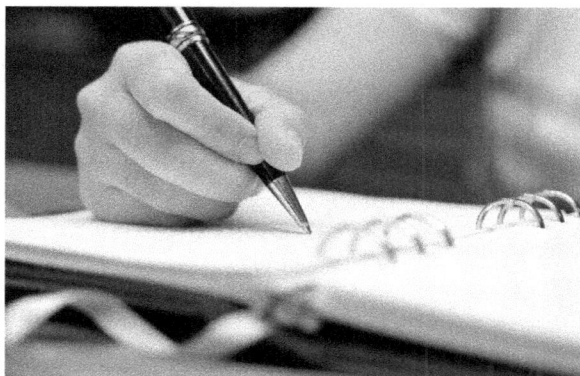

Send a Message with the Firebowl

"Minds are like parachutes. They only function when they are open."
~ James Dewar

Time Required: Sixty Minutes

The Firebowl is a magical tool that you can use psychically for divination and for other purposes such as to communicate with higher powers and beings. This recipe gives you directions on constructing your own Firebowl and then instructions on how to use it to send and receive messages and information from the Universe.

Ingredients

- Sun Yellow candle
- A charged Firebowl that is made of brass, cast-iron, ceramic or a hard hardwood, 4-6 inches in diameter and 4-5 inches deep, with a shape that is easily held with one or both hands and light enough to carry in

one hand if necessary, that will be stable when placed on a flat surface, and that the shape of the bowl curves-in and flares back out at the top rim to promote "columning" of incense or smoke

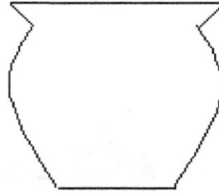

- Ground fire clay or clean, fine sand. Non-scented cat litter, which is ground fire clay, works well for this as long as it does not have chemicals or deodorants in it
- Self-starting charcoal discs, which can be purchased from religious supply stores or online. The round charcoals with bowl-shaped depressions in the middle are best. The pie shaped depressions don't work as well
- Wooden or paper matches. Use only wooden or paper matches to light your candles and charcoals. The scent and energetic side-bands associated with butane and other petroleum products change the fire-bands you're working with
- Finely chopped or shaved wood chips or tree bark to insulate the charcoal from tree resins or incense and to facilitate the burning of the materials in your Firebowl
- Pine resin that you can collect yourself or purchase
- Finely ground or rubbed sage

Recipe Directions
1. Fill the bottom of the Firebowl with 1-2 inches of sand or clay.

2. Place a self-starting charcoal disc in the center of the bed of sand or clay.

3. Have your wood shavings, sage, and resin ready to put onto the charcoal after it is lit. Make sure your pine resin is broken into small pieces that can be easily added onto the wood shavings.

4. Light your Sun Yellow candle with wooden or paper matches and charge it by cupping your hands over the flame once the flame of the candle is burning tall and bright (called a working flame), and say the following litany in a voice of command:

"Child of Wonder
Child of Flame
Nourish My Spirit
And Bring My Aim."

5. Stand or sit in the South facing North with your Firebowl and materials in front of you.

6. Light the charcoal from the flame of your Sun Yellow candle. The charcoal will begin sparking within seconds. If the charcoal is old or damp, you may need to use tongs to hold it over the flame for several minutes. Also, with old or damp charcoal, you may want to light the top of it in the center of the bowl-shaped depression so that the materials you put on top will burn more easily.

7. Once the charcoal is lit in the center of your Firebowl, blow Sun Yellow energy, pulled from your candle, into it.

8. Add wood shavings to the charcoal, then pine resin, then sage as needed until the Firebowl is producing a good column of smoke.

9. In a voice of command charge the Firebowl with the

verse below, blowing Sun Yellow into the charcoal before you start, between each line and after you complete the verse.

"Fire and Air where you are cast,
Let no spell nor adverse purpose last,
Not in accord with me!
Send this message to powers and beings above,
That they may hear my request and manifest it with love.
Thus my will, so it be!"

10. The smoke from a Firebowl can literally carry your message upward, to powers and beings "above" us in the hierarchy. To communicate with higher powers and beings, first write your message on a clean White or Sky Blue sheet of paper.

11. Then light your paper request and drop it in the Firebowl. The smoke from your burnt request will mingle with the Firebowl smoke and carry your message to higher powers and beings.

How to Use the Results of Your Recipe

You can also use the charged Firebowl to receive messages and information from higher sources and to clear your space of junky or negative energies that can interfere with your receiving of information. Change the charge verse in these cases to:

"Fire and Air where you are cast,
Let no spell nor adverse purpose last,
Not in accord with me.
Cleanse these walls and cleanse this space,
Far from here send baneful trace.
Thus my will, so it be."

The Firebowl used this way can provide you with a direct method of divination in that it gives you a visual field that the mind can visually project the information you are seeking. Direct divination methods allow psychic or unconscious perceptions to manifest into the five senses so we can understand them more easily. As you peer into the smoke, hold an image of a person or object connected to the information you are seeking and/or get very curious about the topic, question, person, or object. You can ask questions to increase your feeling of curiosity such as "Where is...?", "Where was I in [name of time period]?", or "What is likely to happen if I...?". Peer into the column of smoke and look for images or visual clues to form. Some people find it easier to close their eyes when looking into the smoke to keep visual distraction out. If you get an image, but not in enough detail to make sense to you, keep asking questions until it becomes clearer or you can ask the image to zoom in or out, shift left or shift right so that you can see more details in the "picture".

[this page is intentionally left blank]

More Magickal Resources

Kindle or Paperback on Amazon:
1. *Witchcraft Spell Book Series:*
- Learn How to Do Witchcraft Rituals and Spells with Your Bare Hands (Witchcraft Spell Books, Book 1)
- Learn How to Do Witchcraft Rituals and Spells with Household Ingredients (Witchcraft Spell Books, Book 2)
- Learn How to Do Witchcraft Rituals and Spells with Magical Tools (Witchcraft Spell Books, Book 3)
- Witchcraft Spell Book: The Complete Guide of Witchcraft Rituals & Spells for Beginners (compilation of Books 1, 2, & 3)

2. *Kitchen Table Magick Series*

Ebooks and Online Courses at *www.shamanschool.com*
- Wand: Air Tool
- Athame: Fire Tool
- Chalice: Water Tool
- Plate: Earth Tool
- Magical Tool: Firebowl
- Psychic Development
- Energy Healing For Self and Others

- How to Do Voodoo
- Daily Rituals to Attract What You Want in Life

Find a complete list of magickal resources on https://amzn.to/3swxvPo. These resources are constantly updated so check back often!

Free Gift Offer

To thank you for purchasing this book, I'd like to give you a

100% FREE GIFT

Learn more about your free magickal gift.

Access Your Free Gift at www.shamanschool.com

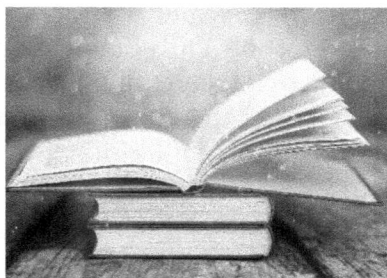

Find a complete list of magickal resources on https://amzn.to/3swxvPo. These resources are constantly updated so check back often!

About G. Alan Joel

Magick means many things to different people. The form of magick taught by G. Alan Joel for more than 30 years is steeped in tribal traditions from around the world, from both modern tribal cultures and those from the past, which have been mostly passed on through oral dialog.

At the very heart of the magick that Mr. Joel teaches is the use of Universal Laws for the benefit of self, others, and even the planet. These magickal traditions can take on many forms, including simple rituals for daily use, specific spells for particular life situations, the use of simulacra (often better known as voodoo), weather working, water witching, the use of the elemental tools (Firebowl, Wand, Athame, Chalice, and Plate), magickal self-defense rituals, and more. Also included are the use of the Tarot for divination and spellwork, divination rituals of all kinds, Spirit-to-Spirit communication, exercises for psychic development, and abundant healing techniques.

Through his 30 plus years of studying, teaching, and honing his magickal practice, G. Alan Joel has helped thousands of people successfully integrate the magickal, and seemingly miraculous, into their daily lives. In fact, one of the greatest gifts Mr. Joel has offered through his teachings is the ability for his students to always find a magickal solution for life situations that often seem impossible to solve. With magick, anything is possible in the mundane world. All that is required of the practitioner is an open mind, the desire to learn, and a willingness to pay some time and effort into his or her magickal practice. One of Mr. Joel's favorite quotes is:

"What you pay into your practice pays you back!"

While many magickal traditions have fiercely guarded their secrets from the public, Mr. Joel feels that "Magick is the birthright of every planetary citizen." As such he strives to offer magickal teachings that are easily learned and inexpensive (no excessive fees to join exclusive magickal groups or ascend up the levels of learning). He also offers techniques that are usable and effective for all who are sincere in their desire to practice magick. In essence, Mr. Joel's methods teach a form of "Every Man's (and Woman's) Magick." All are welcome, his teachings are simple yet effective, and he also offers online classes in which he helps students troubleshoot their magickal issues in an interactive setting.

Find out more about Mr. Joel's teachings here and on his website (***www.shamanschool.com***) where magickal offerings are updated on a regular basis.

Mr. Joel augments this magickal knowledge and teaching with 30 years of practice as Doctor of Chinese Medicine, including a deep understanding of herbology and acupuncture. His understanding of the healing arts deepens the magickal knowledge he teaches, as magickal healing is a major aspect of his teachings. Mr. Joel believes that while there is clearly a time and place for Western Medicine, magickal and Eastern healing techniques can be harmoniously blended in to offer people many choices for healing all types of health conditions.

About the Esoteric School of Shamanism and Magic

The Esoteric School of Shamanism and Magic was started from a desire for all people from all over the globe to be able to attend a real, if virtual, school dedicated to magick and shamanism. The aim of the Esoteric School of Shamanism and Magic is to help people create permanent, positive change in their lives through the study of esoteric magickal and shamanic knowledge. It doesn't matter what your esoteric background is, whether you started out with witchcraft, religious studies, spirituality or candle magick, we welcome you. We believe that the Truth is the same, no matter which form you practice. We delight in all manner of shamanic schools and traditions, magickal techniques and esoteric ritual. You can visit us at ***www.shamanschool.com***, our blog at ***http://shamanmagic.blogspot.com***, or on social media via links on our website.

[this page intentionally left blank]

[this page intentionally left blank]

[this page intentionally left blank]

[this page intentionally left blank]